DRUGS AND SEX

Relationships based on shared responsibilities and mutual respect are usually strong and lasting.

THE DRUG ABUSE PREVENTION LIBRARY

DRUGS AND SEX

George A. Boyd

THE ROSEN PUBLISHING GROUP, INC.
NEW YORK

The people pictured in this book are only models; they in no way practice or endorse the activities illustrated. Captions serve only to explain the subjects of the photographs and do not imply a connection between real-life models and the staged situations shown. News agency photographs are exceptions.

Published in 1994 by The Rosen Publishing Group, Inc.
29 East 21st Street, New York, NY 10010

First Edition

Manufactured in the United States of America

Library of Congress Cataloging-in-Publication Data

Boyd, George A.
    Drugs and sex / by George A. Boyd.
      p.   cm. (Drug abuse prevention library)
    Includes bibliographical references and index.
      ISBN 0-8239-1538-7
      1. Teenagers—United States—Drug use—Juvenile
      literature. 2. Teenagers—United States—Drug
      use—Prevention—Juvenile literature. 3. Drug
      abuse—United States—Juvenile literature. 4. Sex
      instruction for teenagers—United States. 5.
      Drugs and sex—United States—Juvenile litera-
      ture. 6. Safe sex in AIDS prevention—United
      States—Juvenile literature. [1. Drug abuse.
      2. Sex instruction for youth. 3. Drugs and sex.
      4. Sexually transmitted diseases.] I. Title.
      II. Series.
      HV5824.Y68B69   1993
      613.9—dc20   93-5873
                                                  CIP
                                                    AC

Contents

Knowing and understanding each other will help a couple to make responsible decisions.

CHAPTER 1

An Overview of the Problem

*H*aving sex is an important decision that needs careful thought. Whether you believe in abstinence (no sex at all) or believe in safe sex (using condoms) with a loved one, the effect drugs or drink can have on your beliefs is negative. Mind-altering substances impair judgment. Having sex can lead to serious consequences. You want to have a clear mind when making such an important choice. This book is about the effects of drugs, what happens when you have sex, and what happens when you mix the two.

Once a boy or girl reaches *puberty*, having sex can produce babies. Puberty is the age when the body changes to allow males and females to create a new life. Girls

8 begin to develop breasts to nurse a baby and begin to release eggs (ovulate). Boys begin to produce sperm and semen. Boys and girls begin to notice the opposite sex strongly at this time. They develop a powerful urge to have sex. The sex drive is nature's way of making sure that human beings continue to have babies so that the species will survive.

Sometimes the urge to have sex can be so strong that a boy and girl may not think about possible consequences. Without some kind of contraception (birth control), the girl can become pregnant.

Pregnancy can cause a young girl and her family many problems. It is very expensive to raise babies to adulthood. They must be fed and clothed, must receive medical care and education, and be given love and attention. In 1991, it was estimated that the cost to raise one child through high school was at least $151,170. Sometimes a girl who becomes pregnant must give up schooling or job training to care for her baby. She may have to give up many of her dreams for her life.

A girl's pregnancy can also affect the boy who makes her pregnant. He may have to take a low-paying job to help with expenses. He may be unable to finish high school and go to college. He may never earn as much money as if he had completed school.

If the girl or boy or their families cannot support the child, they may have to apply for welfare. That is really not enough to live on, but it may have to do until the baby is old enough for the mother to get a job and help support the family. But it is hard to find someone to care for the baby.

Today, there are many ways to prevent pregnancy, including condoms, the pill, an IUD, contraceptive sponges, Norplant (a chemical contraceptive), or a diaphragm.

STDs

Another serious consequence of having sex is the risk of passing or contracting a sexually transmitted disease (STD). Some STDs, like AIDS (acquired immunodeficiency syndrome), have no cure and can be fatal. Herpes also cannot be cured, and it can cause harm to a newborn baby. Other STDs such as chlamydia, gonorrhea, and NGU (nongonoccal urethritis) may damage reproductive organs. Gonorrhea may lead to heart trouble, brain damage, insanity, and death. People who have an STD may not know they have it. You are

10 at real risk of catching it if you do not use some method of protection such as a condom.

AIDS is the most dangerous of the STDs. This frightening disease attacks your immune system. It prevents your body from protecting itself from bacteria and viruses, and it can eventually kill you. AIDS can be spread by having sex with a boy or girl who has human immunodeficiency virus (HIV), from injecting drugs with an infected needle, or by contact with contaminated blood products.

More teenagers are getting AIDS than any other group, so it is very important that you protect yourself. To be sure you don't catch HIV, you must avoid risky drug and sex contacts. The best way to avoid the risk is not to use drugs, especially those that are injected. However, if you do inject drugs, never shoot drugs with another person's syringe. The only truly safe way to avoid catching AIDS from sexual contact is abstinence. If you do have sex, you are safer if you always use a condom with nonoxynol-9. You also lower your risk of STDs if you practice *monogamy*. Monogamy means having sex with only one person who has sex only with you.

It is wise to be fully informed about the risks of unprotected sex or drug use.

12 *Purple Haze*

In the 1960s, a musician named Jimi Hendrix wrote the song "Purple Haze." Later, a hallucinogenic drug called LSD was sold as "Purple Haze." Some people claimed to have had mystical experiences using LSD. Others went insane.

Throughout history many different peoples have used certain substances that affect the brain and change the state of consciousness. Some cultures consider certain types of drugs acceptable. Many cultures use them in religious ceremonies. Other drugs, however, are considered illegal or taboo. In North America and Europe, alcohol, caffeine, and tobacco are legal drugs. In South America, people chew coca leaves and smoke or inhale cohoba, a powerful hallucinogen. In Arabia, people drink khat, a stimulant made from a shrub. In the Middle East and Far East, hashish and opium are smoked and eaten. The Pacific Islanders drink kava kava. In Southeast Asia and Indonesia, people chew betel nuts. Aboriginal peoples of Siberia and North and Central America have used hallucinogenic mushrooms, cactuses such as psilocybin and peyote, and tobacco at celebrations and in religious rites.

Dangers of Drugs

Just because certain drugs are legal and often socially acceptable in certain cultures does not mean they are safe. Smoking tobacco over long periods can lead to heart disease, cancer, lung disease, and high blood pressure. Drinking alcohol for a long time can lead to liver disease, heart trouble, and stomach problems. It may also be linked to developing cancer.

Illegal drugs pose even bigger and more immediate health risks. Snorting or smoking cocaine can lead to heart attacks, strokes, or seizures. Injecting drugs like heroin, methedrine, and cocaine is dangerous in itself, but sharing the needle can also spread AIDS, hepatitis, and infections of the heart. And an intravenous drug overdose can kill. Use of PCP or hallucinogenic drugs like LSD, mescaline, or peyote can make a person become temporarily or permanently insane.

Social Use of Drugs

Unfortunately, in the United States and many other countries drugs are often used socially. When people use drugs to feel more relaxed and free, it is called lowering inhibitions. Our inhibitions include our morals (beliefs about what is right or

Drugs can affect judgment at school, on the job, or on the road.

wrong), our judgments (decisions about what is appropriate in a certain situation), and our healthy fears (our sense that certain things are too risky). We learn about inhibitions from our parents, our teachers, our religious leaders, and through our own experiences. Inhibitions can sometimes protect us from harm.

Lowering inhibitions can seem like fun at a party, but it can cause serious problems during and after the party. If a boy becomes drunk or high on drugs, his behavior may suddenly change for the worse. He could become violent and start a fight or even kill someone. A boy who is out of control may rape or sexually molest someone. If a girl gets drunk or high, she might have sex against her better judgment. She may even become pregnant or get an STD. People who are high may damage property, spraying paint on walls or breaking windows. People who drive drunk are far more likely to be involved in traffic accidents that cause death and injury. It is estimated that half of all fatal traffic accidents are caused by people who are drunk or high.

People who use alcohol or drugs moderately at a party are called social users. People who use enough to lose many of their inhibitions and cause injury to themselves or other people are called problem users or abusers. And people who completely lose their ability to control their use of drugs are called addicts. Addicts feel driven by their craving for the drug and do things that are against their better judgment. Even though they want to stop using, they can't.

Addiction

Excessive use of drugs and alcohol over a long period of time leads to deterioration. Deterioration means beginning to fall

16 apart physically and mentally. Addicts may no longer be able to hold a job because they are too ill or too obsessed with getting more drugs or alcohol. Addicts may lose their health and strength and develop chronic diseases. So much money is spent on drugs and alcohol that they may become homeless and destitute. They may begin to lose control of their mind and emotions. They may lose memory or even go completely crazy. Continued criminal behavior because of drugs can make people spend much of their lives in prison.

Unchecked abuse of drugs or alcohol ultimately leads to premature death for the substance abuser. Use of drugs and alcohol forms a continuous line from no use (abstinence) to death.

But the bigger picture is that abuse and addiction also cause serious problems for the family, the friends, the employers, and the teachers of the abuser. For every abuser of drugs or alcohol, eight or ten other people may be hurt by it.

NO USE
➥ SOCIAL USE
➥ PROBLEM USE
➥ ADDICTION
➥ DETERIORATION
➥ DEATH

A drug user very often loses control over his or her life.

18 | *Out of Your Mind*

Neurotransmitters are chemicals in the nerve cells in your brain that tell your body how to function. When the body and mind are healthy, the neurotransmitters allow you to think and express your emotions, and to have enough energy to complete your goals. Neurotransmitters are strengthened by vitamins, minerals, proteins, carbohydrates, and fats from the food you eat. When there are too many or two few neurotransmitters, serious mental and physical deterioration takes place.

Neurotransmitters are affected by intoxication. Intoxication happens when the normal functioning of the nervous system is changed by introducing a toxic substance, like a drug, into the bloodstream. Once in the bloodstream, the drug is carried to the brain. There it interacts with neurotransmitters, which is what makes the drug affect you.

When people become intoxicated, they lose much of their self-control. The changes that take place in mind and body cause them to risk harming themselves or others. They lose coordination and poise. Their senses and perceptions of the world are distorted. Their intuition, judgment, and moral senses are all impaired. Will-power is weakened. People can tempo-rarily become completely out of control mentally, emotionally, and physically.

Sometimes other people, like friends, can strongly influence a person's values and beliefs. People can sometimes be pressured into doing things that are not in their own best interests. Friends can give them false ideas to justify doing things that harm themselves and others. When people take drugs, they stop functioning in a normal state of consciousness. They might do something that could affect them for the rest of their lives.

The Life-Changing Choice

As you have read, if you want to engage in sex, you need to understand the risks. One sexual encounter can make you the parent of a child, which you are probably not ready to care for or support. One sexual encounter can give you AIDS, which can kill you. One sexual encounter may change the relationship between you and your partner—a friend, an acquaintance, or a boyfriend or girlfriend. Having sex is a life-changing choice.

Many feelings are linked with having sex. Guys and girls may think they are in

Every girl has the right and responsibility to make her own decisions about sex.

love and want to be more intimate with each other. They sometimes feel awkward about the entire subject of sex. They may be confused about whether it is all right to have sex, or whether they should wait until they are married. They may want to abstain from sex, but feel pressure from their friends to do it.

Some girls feel ashamed and angry at themselves when they lose their virginity. They may come to think of themselves as bad, or feel depressed because they have a

terrible, shameful secret. But having a
sexual relationship with someone special
can be wonderful. You must, however,
fully understand what you are doing, why
you are doing it, and take responsibility
for the consequences.

Guys often feel proud that they have
had sex. But they often worry whether
they have made the girl pregnant or if
they've caught a disease. Guys also worry
about their sexual performance. They
might feel ashamed if they happen to
ejaculate too quickly or if they have problems getting an erection. But guys need to
consider the same things as girls when
thinking about having sex. They need to
be sure of what they are getting themselves into by knowing the consequences
of sexual contact and learning how to protect themselves.

The decisions about sex become even
harder when people add drugs to the equa-
tion. Drugs make people think they are in
a fantasy. They forget about consequences
and act on impulse.

The decision to have sex evokes many
deep feelings. Learn more about sexuality
and its role in your life. You may choose
to abstain from sex until you are ready to
handle the responsibility involved.

Many drugs alter perceptions and create a distorted view of surrounding objects.

CHAPTER 2

What Drugs Do to Your Body

*D*rugs have a powerful effect on your body. Because drugs affect several neurotransmitters, they upset the balance of these chemicals in your brain and other organs. The body strives to achieve and maintain *homeostasis*. Homeostasis is the right amount of chemicals in your body to help you cope with the demands of day-to-day living and to enjoy life. The effects of neurotransmitters are explained in more detail on page 25.

Each drug has its own signature in the way it affects the body. It also breaks down in a unique way, which allows scientists to detect the breakdown of products

24 of each drug as it shows up in the blood or the urine. This means that if a person takes a drug, within a certain time it can be detected by special tests of the blood or urine.

Drugs that make people sleepy and lower inhibitions are called *sedative drugs*. Examples of sedative drugs are alcohol, barbiturates, Quaaludes, and Valium.

Drugs that make people more alert, give them energy, and increase their feelings of confidence are called *stimulant drugs*. Cigarettes, coffee, cola, amphetamines, and cocaine are types of stimulant drugs.

Drugs that ease pain and put people into euphoric and dreamy states of mind are called *narcotic drugs*. Narcotic drugs such as opium, heroin, morphine, codeine, and hydrocodone often are abused.

Drugs that distort people's time perception and alter their thinking are called *hallucinogens*. Marijuana, LSD, peyote, phencyclidine (PCP, angel dust) and psilocybin mushrooms create powerful visual illusions and states of confusion.

Effects of Drugs on Sexual Behavior
John met Linda at his school in Kansas City. He asked her to a party on Saturday night at his friend Bill's house.

EFFECTS OF NEUROTRANSMITTERS

NEURO-TRANSMITTER	TOO MUCH	RIGHT AMOUNT	TOO LITTLE
Gamma amino butric acid	Coma	Self-control, calmness	Convulsions, anxiety
Dopamine	Insanity	Coordinated movement	Uncontrolled movement
Norepinephrine	Mania	Confidence	Depression, no pleasure or motivation
Acetylcholine	Convulsions, delirium	Good memory, normal muscle activity	Paralysis, loss of memory
Adrenaline	Fear, panic, paranoia	Energy for daily living and sex	Exhaustion, no energy
Serotonin	Feelings of acuity of senses; distortion of senses; omnipotence	Normal dreaming	Insomnia
Endorphin	Euphoria, coma	Pain control, sense of reward for achievements	Low pain tolerance, misery, no sex pleasure
Glutamic acid	Headaches, obsessive thoughts	Concentration and thinking	Inability to concentrate or think clearly
Sex hormones	Uncontrollable sex drive	Normal sex drive and enjoyment	No sex drive, impotence

Bill's parents were away for the weekend. Bill's older brother, who was left to supervise, was out with his girlfriend. Bill took a knife and pried open his parents' liquor cabinet. Soon he was playing loud rock music on the stereo and pouring beer, wine, and whiskey for all his friends.

25

26   *John and Linda had some wine and beer. John was starting to get drunk, and Linda felt giddy. After a few dances, John suggested they go into the back bedroom. Linda agreed and soon they were kissing and touching each other.*

In the back of Linda's mind, she could hear her parents and Sunday school teacher warning her about having sex. But she was feeling so good that she ignored the voices. That night Linda "went all the way." She lost her virginity.

Some drugs may make the user do dangerous things.

The next day, Linda awoke with a headache and had pain in her vagina. She felt ashamed and angry at herself for having sex outside of marriage. She was afraid that people would find out and call her names.

Linda's shame and anxiety increased when she missed her period several weeks later. She went to the school nurse and had a pregnancy test; it was positive. Linda had to decide whether to have an abortion or to become a mother at age 14.

John did not take it well when he found out Linda was pregnant. He worried that he would have to quit school and get a job. He feared that Linda's parents might hit him with a paternity suit. John become anxious. He had trouble sleeping; he lost his appetite, and he began to do poorly in his schoolwork.

Sedatives

Sedative drugs like alcohol, Quaaludes, or Valium lower people's inhibitions. This makes them more likely to act upon their sex desires. However, these drugs can also lower sex performance and enjoyment because they tend to deaden or anesthetize the senses. If a boy and girl have sex while they are drunk, the boy may have trouble getting and keeping an erection or may

28 ejaculate too soon. The girl may not feel any pleasure from the sex act or fail to have an orgasm.

Stimulants

Strong stimulants such as cocaine or methamphetamine may temporarily increase the sex drive. If people take them repeatedly, however, the drugs begin to have the opposite effect. People who continue to use cocaine or methamphetamine lose their sex drive and their capacity to enjoy sex. After even longer periods of time, they may start to have bizarre sex fantasies and frightening delusions that people are out to harm them, or that insects are crawling under their skin.

Narcotics

Narcotic drugs put people into a sleepy, dreamy state of mind. These drugs lower sexual desire, and long-term use of narcotics may make a boy impotent. Because they interfere with endorphins, they can cause problems with having an orgasm.

Hallucinogens

Mild hallucinogenic drugs such as kava kava or marijuana can relax people. They may also distort and sometimes seem to

Safe sex with condom protection is one way to avoid an unwanted pregnancy and the danger of catching a sexually transmitted disease.

30 | enhance their senses. When the senses of sight, hearing, taste, smell, and touch are enhanced, pleasure can become more intense. But the distortion of sensation at the same time may make sex acts seem disgusting, strange, or weird.

Stronger hallucinogens like LSD or peyote can create profound illusions of the senses. Some people who have sex while under their influence experience terrifying thoughts and feelings about sex.

Effects of Drugs Over Time

Drugs are poison to the body. When people keep taking drugs, they damage the cells of their organ systems. Drugs kill brain cells, which lowers the ability to remember, to think clearly, and make sound judgments. Drugs damage the liver, which makes it harder for the body to purify harmful substances. Drugs like cocaine can damage the heart and blood vessels, putting people at risk for heart attack or stroke. Drugs can weaken the kidneys. This keeps more poisons in the bloodstream, which makes all the other organs have to work harder. Drugs can attack the lungs, making it difficult to breathe. Drugs lower the immune system, making users more likely to become ill. Drugs steal

vitamins and minerals from the body, **31**
making users more likely to show signs of
vitamin and mineral deficiency and of
early aging. Drugs seriously affect the reproductive system. Drugs can stop a girl's
periods and interfere with hormone production and ovulation. They can lower the
amount of sex hormones in a boy's blood
and can make his testes atrophy, or waste
away. If a girl is pregnant, drugs can damage the unborn baby.

Drugs are dangerous "invaders" that
take your body a long time to eliminate.
The body of a person addicted to sedative
and narcotic drugs undergoes physical
withdrawal symptoms when the drug is
stopped. The addicted person feels sick
and miserable for weeks. Withdrawal
from sleeping pills, tranquilizers, or alcohol can even make people go into seizures
or give them terrifying nightmares.

Drugs ultimately destroy the health of
those who take them. But what drugs do
to the mind is even more dangerous than
what they do to the body.

Drugs or alcohol tend to lower inhibitions and may cause
people to make reckless decisions.

CHAPTER 3

Effects of Drugs on the Mind

Eduardo was spending more and more time with his friends after school. He felt he really belonged, that they understood him. He could be himself with them. He wanted to be liked and accepted, and when they suggested he smoke cigarettes and drink beer on weekends to be "cool," he went right along.

Later on, one of the boys brought a glass pipe with white crystals of crack cocaine and started smoking. Eduardo tried smoking the crack. For a few minutes he felt omnipotent—powerful, confident, as if nothing could harm him—and then the feeling went away. He liked the feeling and smoked more crack to try to get it back. Soon, Eduardo was smoking crack regularly on weekends.

34

His friends also liked to brag how far they had gone with their girlfriends. One guy had gone all the way—had sex with his girlfriend, a virgin—and all the other boys in the group were envious. Eduardo was curious about sex but felt a little scared and worried about actually doing it.

One night at a party, after a few drinks, Eduardo met Maria. Maria kept smiling and looking at him, and Eduardo knew she liked him. After dancing for a while, they went off to a bedroom together and started necking. Eduardo was feeling excited, but also a little nervous.

Then someone brought a crack pipe into the next room. Eduardo smelled it and excused himself to go and smoke some. The feelings of omnipotence came back. He felt confident, as if he could do anything. He went back to necking with Maria and now started touching her genitals. She pulled his hand away and told him strongly to stop it. Eduardo thought of how envious his friends would be if he went all the way. Ignoring her protests, he pulled Maria down on the bed and tried to force her to have sex. Maria wrestled free and ran out of the room, crying. She was confused and scared. Eduardo, feeling powerful under the influence of cocaine, had nearly raped Maria.

David

David moved with his wealthy parents to a suburb of New York City. He smoked heroin with his new friends at school. David liked the mellow, dreamy feeling it gave him, so he used it more and more. One day, he awoke to find himself drenched in sweat, with bone-shaking chills and terrible stomach cramps. David had become addicted to heroin. He was having withdrawal pains.

David started stealing money from his parents and shoplifting from stores to buy heroin. His habit was growing. He needed to inject heroin four times a day to avoid being sick. David was very ashamed of himself for stealing, which was against his upbringing, but he rationalized that it was necessary to keep him from going through withdrawal.

David's girlfriend, Beth, liked to make love with him. But as David used more heroin, he started having trouble getting and keeping an erection. He began to lose interest in sex. Beth was understanding; she said it was nice just to be held by him. But then David stopped seeing Beth and gave no explanation. When Beth asked him why, David made up stories. Beth was worried; she knew he was changing.

36

David's parents, too, noticed that he was spending more and more time by himself. They asked what was troubling him, and he insisted that nothing was wrong. David was now in strong denial that he had a drug problem.

Later, when expensive things started disappearing from their house, David's parents came to suspect that he had a problem with drugs. When they confronted David, he loudly denied that he was stealing from them or using drugs. He said they didn't love or care about him and didn't trust him. David blamed his parents instead of looking at his own actions. Without help, David could not admit that he had a problem. Instead, he began to feel paranoid, thinking that his parents were against him and would turn him over to the police. This made him isolate himself even more.

Drugs deadened David's feelings and made him forget his morals. Drugs also made David fool himself by using fantasy modes of thinking—rationalization, denial, displacement, projection, and paranoia. He could no longer identify what he was feeling. He distorted his parents' loving concern and thought they were out to harm him.

Dewaine

Dewaine, a young man in South Central Los Angeles, dropped out of high school in his second year and couldn't find work. He felt frustrated and angry. He blamed society for not providing a job for him and for making school so boring that he came to hate it. He hung out every day on the city streets, drinking malt liquor and smoking crack. He shrugged off his mother's constant criticism and he talked about his future with his friends.

Drug use may lower sexual desire and ruin relationships.

38

Dewaine's girlfriend, Latasha, was very supportive. She tried to give him hope that he would find work if he kept looking. Latasha had a special reason for wanting Dewaine to work. After months of unprotected sex with him, Latasha believed she was pregnant.

Latasha was also frightened by what she saw happening to Dewaine. He would get drunk and drive so recklessly that she was afraid to ride with him. He was also absent for long periods of time and couldn't give her a satisfactory explanation. She began to worry that Dewaine might be sleeping with other girls—and she was right. She also worried that when she had her baby, Dewaine wouldn't stay with her.

Using drugs had begun to affect Dewaine's judgment and thinking. He thought he could handle driving and drinking. He was no longer concerned about the consequences of having unprotected sex, or how he would care for his girlfriend if she became pregnant. He was not considering how Latasha might feel if he slept with other girls. He didn't anticipate what might happen if he caught an STD from one of those girls and gave it to Latasha and their unborn child.

Drugs make people feel omnipotent, lead them into fantasy modes of thinking, impair their judgment, and distort their ability to recognize emotions. Drugs make users lose touch with reality. They no longer realize the consequences of their actions. Under the influence of drugs, they harm others and themselves.

When they become addicted to drugs, guys and girls may trade sex for drugs or even become prostitutes to support a drug habit. As a result, they have many sex partners. When they are "drug sick" and desperate, they fail to use condoms while having sex. This places them at the highest risk to catch STDs, including AIDS, and to spread these diseases to others.

During the 1960s, in the era of "hippies" and "free love," the use of marijuana, LSD, and methamphetamine led people to have sex with many more partners. This led to the largest increase of STDs that was ever recorded. It also led to many more teenage pregnancies than in any previous generation. But even with all the research, information, and warnings about STDs and teen pregnancy today, these statistics are still growing.

Sometimes young people start to drink or smoke because they want to be part of the crowd.

CHAPTER 4

Social Pressures to Use Drugs and Have Sex

*P*eople belong to groups from an early age. The earliest group is made up of your parents and brothers and sisters, your family group. Later you become a member of groups at school: learning groups, classrooms with the same people, and groups of friends. You may join clubs or hobby groups, or compete in sports. There may be group activities and clubs in your religion. There are work groups on the job and social gatherings of your co-workers that allow you to make new friends and acquaintances.

When you belong to a group, you get certain needs met. Other people make you feel that you belong. They make you feel appreciated and special, and that builds

41

42 your self-esteem. You might be able to talk to the members of your group about intimate things that you can't tell your parents. People in a group come to know one another and share their thoughts and feelings. You may come to trust and rely on members of your group to stand with you and give you confidence at difficult times. Most people meet the person they marry through groups, too.

Giving In to Peer Pressure

Groups are not always a positive influence. Groups may pressure you to conform by doing things that are very risky and even against the law. You may be ridiculed and embarrassed if you don't go along.

If you continue not to go along, the group may expel you. The group may spread gossip about you. In some groups, like gangs, being expelled from the group is more dangerous. It may mean you will be beaten up or even killed on sight.

Because people want to be liked by their friends, they may be strongly influenced by them. Sometimes peer pressure will make people act against the values they have learned. They are no longer sure what is the right thing to do. When they feel uncertain, the group members

It takes inner strength and good self-esteem not to give in to peer pressure.

tell them what they should do. In this way, people learn a new value system through a group.

The new values are not always good ones. Groups can pressure people to have sex or use drugs. They can make it seem dumb to go to school or get a job. They can make it seem reasonable to rape, to rob, to steal, or even to kill.

People don't recognize when they join a new group of friends that problems may arise. The group may seem sophisticated, wearing the hippest new clothes and talking really cool. The group may do things that usually older people do—drive cars, smoke cigarettes, drink alcohol, and have sex. They may offer you a chance to be part of the fun.

44 | *Paying the Price*

But what many groups don't tell you is what lies ahead if you do as they do. It is not fun when you end up in jail and become stigmatized with a prison record. It is not exciting when you discover you have contracted HIV by having unprotected sex. It is not sophisticated to realize, like David, that you have become addicted to heroin because you smoked it with your friends. It is not hip to find out, like Dewaine, that because you dropped out of school to be with your friends, you can't get a decent job. It is not cool to ignore the warnings about safe sex and to walk out of the doctor's office one day with the news you are pregnant. Now you have to make some of the hardest decisions of your life.

It is important to think about what your friends are telling you to do. The fact that they do it and tell you it is the thing to do, or everybody else is doing it, doesn't make it right. Take the time to decide for yourself what is right and wrong. Consider the consequences of your choices before it's too late. The wrong choices can ruin your life—or even end it.

CHAPTER 5

Myths about Drugs and Sex

A myth is a mistaken belief. Many people can believe a thing is true and act as if it were true. Nevertheless, they suffer real negative consequences because of their false belief. Acting on a mistaken belief leads to errors in judgment that can result in mistakes, accidents, and even tragedy.

People believe several common myths about sex and drugs.

"It Won't Happen to Me."

This is denial at work, a fantasy mode of thinking. Anything that can happen to you, may happen to you. If Jon caught AIDS having unprotected sex, you can catch it, too. If Sally got pregnant after unprotected sex, you can, too. If Billy was killed by drinking and driving, you can die, too, if you drive while drunk.

46 ## *"Nothing Can Harm Me...I'm Magically Protected" (the Invulnerability Myth).*

You may feel unaffected because you are high on a drug, but the laws of the physical universe have not stopped operating. You can still get AIDS if you share infected needles with others to inject drugs. You can still catch other serious STDs or become pregnant by having sex without protection. No matter what you want to believe, you are putting yourself at risk.

"Doing It Just Once Can't Hurt."

Wrong! You can get pregnant or catch an STD from having unprotected sex just once. People die from strokes and heart attacks by using cocaine just once. You can overdose and die from injecting too much heroin just once. You can go crazy using LSD or PCP just once.

"Using Cocaine or Speed Makes Me a Better Lover."

Some people have reported having better sex for a few weeks. But after that your nervous system becomes depleted of neurotransmitters. You may lose your ability to get an erection and you may even lose interest in sex altogether.

A positive self-image is an attractive quality to the opposite sex.

48

"I Won't Become Addicted If I Use."

Statistics report that, on average, one person out of ten who drinks will become addicted to alcohol. If one parent is addicted, the statistic increases to four in ten. If both parents are addicted, it goes up to seven in ten. Every person who becomes addicted to the legal drugs alcohol and cigarettes started out by using those drugs just once. Every person who becomes addicted to an illegal drug such as heroin or cocaine started by trying it just once. People who become addicted to prescription medications like Valium and sleeping pills often start out by thinking, "If the amount my doctor prescribes for me makes me feel this good, one more should make me feel even better."

"I'm More Sexy When I'm High."

You may feel less inhibited, more relaxed, and more confident when you are high. You may seem to have more energy. But you also have temporarily distorted your senses. Your judgment is impaired. You are less in control of your actions and emotions than you think. You have poorer coordination and balance. Your thinking is less clear. You may not be aware that you are acting dangerously.

"If We Just Touch Each Other, We Won't Go Too Far."

When guys and girls become sexually excited, they often feel overcome by the urge to go all the way—especially if one partner is drunk or high on drugs as Eduardo was. Girls are molested and raped every day because guys who are high or drunk could not control their sexual impulses. When dating, it is important to set firm limits beforehand. It is also important to know when to say no.

"My Partner Doesn't Have an STD."

You usually cannot tell by looking whether your partner has an STD. If you are going to have sex, play it safe. Use a fresh condom with nonoxynol-9. If you are not sure what to do or how you are feeling, don't have sex.

"I'm in Complete Control When I'm High."

It may seem so, but as we have already proven, you are not in control. Half of all fatal traffic accidents are caused by people driving drunk or high on drugs. They thought they were in control when they got behind the wheel. They thought they could handle it—they were dead wrong.

50   "I Always Know When I've Had Enough."

If your thinking and judgment are impaired when you are drunk or high, how will you know? Elvis Presley and Marilyn Monroe both died from an overdose of sleeping pills because they didn't realize they had already taken too many.

"Just One More Time Won't Hurt."

If you escaped addiction somehow the last time you used drugs, the crack you smoke or heroin you inject now may be the one that hooks you. Just one more drink can put you over the legal limit and get you arrested for driving under the influence (DUI). Just one more pill or one more injection can be a fatal overdose. Having sex one more time without a condom can get you pregnant or give you an STD or AIDS.

"It's Cool to Have Sex and Use Drugs."

Because adults you admire—sports heroes, movie stars, and rock musicians—have sex and use drugs, it doesn't place them at any less risk. They become addicted. They overdose. They lose jobs or ruin careers because of drugs. They catch STDs and come down with AIDS. They make using drugs and having lots of sex partners seem

Get to know your partner and discuss your mutual concerns
about sex.

52

glamorous because they are so free, rich, and famous. But the same negative consequences of unprotected sex and drug use happen to them—the same consequences that can happen to you.

"My Friends (Brothers, Sisters, Parents) Do It."

This is rationalization. It may seem to you that they are enjoying themselves, and it doesn't appear to hurt them. So you think it is okay for you to do it. But the fact that your friends or relatives do something doesn't necessarily make it healthy, right, or appropriate for you. Just because bad things haven't happened yet to them, it doesn't mean they won't happen to you. You must examine the consequences and think for yourself. You have the right not to go along with what they are doing.

You can avoid these myths by being aware of them and not letting yourself be fooled by them.

CHAPTER 6

Positive Alternatives and Resources

Sometimes people believe that they have to go along with their friends if they want to be liked. This can make them do things that have harmful consequences. When they do those things, they later feel ashamed or confused about them. To make themselves feel better, they use fantasy modes of thinking, like the one called rationalization. They start believing the myths instead of facing the reality of what could happen if they continue doing the harmful things they are doing.

But there are positive alternatives to these harmful actions.

You can get help to become clean and sober again if you are already abusing drugs or alcohol.

54

You can learn how to resist peer pressure to use drugs and to have sex by recognizing the myths, and standing up for your own sense of values.

You can learn how to get "high" naturally. Going into the quiet and beauty of nature, completing a project you design, creating art or playing music, reading an inspiring book, or praying and meditating can bring deep satisfaction, peace, and joy. You do not need a pill, a fix, or a drink to feel high.

You can heighten your senses and increase your energy by exercising, eating a good diet, relaxing, getting enough rest, doing yoga postures and breathing exercises. You do not need a stimulant to increase your energy.

You can feel more confident and build your self-esteem by successfully reaching the goals you set for yourself, by overcoming your fears and learning to deal with things that worry you. You don't need a drug or a drink to make you feel confident and sure of yourself.

You can think about the consequences of having sex. If you are a girl, what if you got pregnant? Would you keep the child? How would you support it? Would you marry the father of your baby? What

Life can be fun and positive without drugs.

would happen if you had to give up school? If you are a guy, what would you do if you got your girlfriend pregnant? Thinking about the consequences of having sex can prevent crisis in your life. You can talk to a counselor, social worker, or public health nurse at your school or at a clinic like Planned Parenthood if you have problems discussing these subjects with your parents.

You can decide to abstain from sex until you are married. If you do decide to have sex, you can always use protection correctly to prevent pregnancy and avoid catching STDs.

Fact Sheet

- 90 percent of 15- to 19-year-old girls who were involved in crime and who used drugs reported they were sexually active. 52 percent of the same age group who used drugs but did not get involved in crime were sexually active. But only 3 percent of girls who were neither taking drugs nor involved with crime were having sex. Boys of the same age showed similar patterns.

- Teenage girls who get pregnant drink more alcohol, use more drugs, and smoke more cigarettes than girls of their age who don't get pregnant.

- Teenage mothers who use drugs have many more problems with their unborn child than those who don't use drugs.

- Teenage mothers are more likely to drop out of school because of money problems and child care. Teenage marriages are also more likely to end in divorce than other marriages.

- 25 percent of teenagers who used crack cocaine said they regularly traded sex for drugs or for money to buy drugs.

- Four out of ten teenage pregnancies are ended by abortion.

- Boys and girls who take the following risks are much more likely to catch STDs and HIV: (1) not using a condom during sex; (2) exchanging sex for drugs or money; (3) having multiple sexual partners per year; (4) using someone else's needle to inject drugs; and (5) taking drugs or drinking alcohol and then having sex.

- Half of the girls who used crack cocaine who were tested in New York City were found to be infected with HIV.

- Boys were more than twice as likely and girls were five times as likely to report that they started using drugs before they began having sex.

Help List

Pregnancy and Sexual Problems:
In the Yellow Pages
- Women's Organizations and Services
- Adolescent and Family Counseling

In the White Pages
- Family Service Association
- Planned Parenthood

Write or call
- Planned Parenthood Federation of
    America
  810 Seventh Avenue
  New York, NY 10019
  (212) 541-7800

If you are raped, call
- A Rape Crisis Center
- Rape Crisis Hot Line.

To learn about preventing STDs, call
- Your County Health Center
- Planned Parenthood
- Health Clinics in your city

Drugs and Alcohol:
In the Yellow Pages
- Alcoholism, Drug Abuse
- Counselors
- Hospitals

In the White Pages

- Alcoholics Anonymous
- Al-Anon
- Alateen (Al-Anon will have information about these meetings)
- Cocaine Anonymous
- County Health Services
- Narcotics Anonymous
- National Council of Alcoholism

Write or call

- National Council on Alcoholism
  12 West 21st Street
  New York, NY 10010
  (212) 206-6770
- Alcoholics Anonymous World Services, Inc.
  P.O. Box 459
  Grand Central Station
  New York, NY 10163
- Narcotics Anonymous World Service Office
  16155 Wyandotte Street
  Van Nuys, CA 91406

For support and more information

- Teen hot lines
- County or hospital mental health services
- Your school counseling office
- Your school nurse
- Adolescent counseling clinics

Glossary
Explaining New Words

AIDS (acquired immunodeficiency syndrome) Disease caused by the HIV (human immunodeficiency virus).

delusion False belief that a person insists is true in spite of evidence to the contrary.

denial Fantasy mode of thinking whereby people are no longer aware of their feelings or the consequences of their actions.

displacement Fantasy mode of thinking that blames others for things that go wrong.

hallucinogen Drug that distorts the senses and time perception and alters thinking and the sense of self.

illusion Distortion of the senses; seeing or hearing what actually isn't there.

inhibitions Morals (beliefs about what is right or wrong), judgment (decisions on what is appropriate in a certain situation), and healthy fears (sense that certain things are too risky).

invulnerability The belief that one is magically protected from harm.

myth Mistaken belief that is acted upon as if it were true.

narcotic Drug that lowers pain and induces a euphoric and dreamy state of mind.

neurotransmitters Chemicals in the body by which one nerve cell communicates with another; they are believed to enable people to perform action, to sense the environment, and to feel emotions and formulate thoughts.

omnipotence Belief in a personal power so great that nothing can harm one.

paranoia Mental disorder in which people believe that others intend to harm or betray them.

projection Fantasy mode of thinking that makes a person believe other people have certain intentions toward him when in fact those intentions are the person's own secret fears and worries.

rationalization Effort to explain away or make excuses for actions, instead of taking responsibility.

sedative Drug that induces sleepiness, lessens tension, and lowers inhibitions.

STD (sexually transmitted disease) Disease that can be contracted by sexual relations.

stimulant Drug that makes people more alert, gives them energy, and increases feelings of confidence.

For Further Reading

Calderone, Mary S., MD, and Johnson, Eric W. *The Family Book about Sexuality*. New York: Harper & Row, Publishers, 1981.

Edwards, Gabrielle I. *Coping with Drug Abuse*, rev. ed. New York: Rosen Publishing Group, 1990.

Johnson, Eric W. *Love and Sex in Plain Language*. New York: Bantam Books, 1979.

Johnson, Eric W., and Johnson, Corinne B. *Love and Sex and Growing Up*. New York: Bantam Books, 1979.

Kurland, Adrienne, R.N. *Coping with Being Pregnant*. New York: Rosen Publishing Group, 1988.

Mahoney, Ellen V. *Coping with Safer Sex*. New York: Rosen Publishing Group, 1990.

McFarland, Rhoda. *Coping with Substance Abuse*, rev. ed. New York: Rosen Publishing Group, 1990.

Taylor, Barbara. *Everything You Need to Know about Alcohol*, rev. ed. New York: Rosen Publishing Group, 1993.

Index

About the Author

George A. Boyd is a certified drug counselor. He leads groups for adult children of dysfunctional families and trained groups in meditation. He has also lectured and led workshops on meditation and on drug-abuse recovery. He is also a respected poet.

Photo Credits

Cover: Dick Smolinski.
Page 17: Michael F. O'Brien; page 55: Mary Lauzon; all other photos by Dick Smolinski.

Design & Production: Blackbirch Graphics, Inc.